IDEAS Plus

A Collection of Practical Teaching Ideas

Book Thirteen

The Pearl - 31

Cask of Amontillado p. 36

g.E. p 38

R+J 41

Scarlet Letter p 50

gatby 34

National Council of Teachers of English
1111 W. Kenyon Road, Urbana, Illinois 61801-1096

Project Coordinator: Felice Kaufmann

Copy Editor: Lee Erwin

Staff Editor: Peter Feely

Cover Design: Joellen Bryant

Interior Book Design: Tom Kovacs for TGK Design

NCTE Stock Number: 22744

Library of Congress Catalog Card Number 84-3479

IDEAS Plus is published in August by the National Council of Teachers of
English as an exclusive benefit of NCTE Plus membership. NCTE Plus membership also includes four issues of NOTES Plus (ISSN 0738-86-24), published
in October, December, January, and March. Annual membership dues are
$55.00; $15.00 of this amount is for NOTES Plus and IDEAS Plus. Inquiries
about NCTE Plus membership or communications regarding change of address
and permission to reprint should be addressed to NOTES Plus, 1111 W. Kenyon
Road, Urbana, IL 61801-1096. POSTMASTER: Send address changes to
NOTES Plus, 1111 W. Kenyon Road, Urbana, IL 61801-1096. Second-class
postage paid at Champaign, Illinois, and at additional mailing offices.

Contents

Foreword

IDEAS Plus and its quarterly companion *NOTES Plus* are the principal benefits of *NCTE Plus* membership. *IDEAS Plus* is sent out at the end of the summer so that teachers will have it in hand as they begin the school year.

The ideas collected in this thirteenth edition of *IDEAS Plus* come from two sources: ideas submitted at an Idea Exchange session at an NCTE Annual Convention or Spring Conference, and contributions by readers of *NOTES Plus* and *IDEAS Plus*.

1 Prewriting and Writing

We know that student writers, like all writers, need techniques that can help them focus their ideas, get the words flowing, and then stand back and read their writing the way others might. And we also know that students need, perhaps most of all, to feel the confidence and excitement that come with writing from their own experiences, convictions, and creative inspirations. The activities that follow draw on classic works of art, illustrated books, personal memories, a mysterious collection of objects, and the newspaper stories that students see every day to stimulate their thinking and generate writing that they can really call their own.

Rich Associations Lead to Poetry

Sometimes our students need a chance to fantasize, to dream about other lives and other times. This activity allows students to explore different voices, to assume the dramatic elements of masquerade, and to experience the liberation of other personae. It works best if done in a single class session, and takes an hour or an hour and a half.

Gather at least ten more dress-up items than you have students in one class. I've used an assortment of 1940s hand-painted ties and old silk scarves simply because I own them and they're small enough to bring to school easily. Other teachers who have adapted this activity have brought in everything from a shoebox full of costume jewelry to piles of old hats and gowns. Students' fanciful associations seem richer if they are unfamiliar with both the items and the era when they were manufactured. Have the items spread out on display when students arrive. Ask them to walk around and to look at all of the pieces before selecting one. Stress that they should pick items that appeal to them not because they would like to own them but because they have begun to imagine who might have once worn them, what "adventures" the items might have been involved in.

Once they are seated with the chosen objects, the students will need only writing tools. If time permits, allow students a few moments to contemplate their items. Now, they're ready to write. As they do, encourage them to hold on to the objects—the tactile closeness aids association. Some students readily don the belongings. When students are ready to write, give them the following guidelines, pausing after each to let them write.

1. Examine your object as if you were a detective. Look at its every detail objectively. Use specific sensory details to describe it accurately and thoroughly. Be as complete as you would need to be if you were presenting the object as evidence in a case.
2. You are the curator of a museum. As such, you have been assigned to create the exhibit card to accompany this object in a display. Assume that you have complete knowledge of the origin and history of this object. Write the exhibit card, highlighting important or interesting moments in the object's history.
3. Now, become the item's owner, or its most important owner if it has had more than one. Or you may be the person who created it, if you'd rather. Consider how you felt about this thing: Why did you value it? In what way did it affect your life? Imagine the most important day in its time with you. Write a journal entry for that day.
4. Quickly imagine and record answers to these: Where did you acquire this item? Where did you keep it? What else was nearby? What are its secrets? Its powers?
5. Reread what you've written. Focus on the phrases or lines which most intrigue you. Use them as a starting point to draft a poem.

Deirdre G. Callanan, Dennis-Yarmouth Administration Center, South Yarmouth, Massachusetts

Growling Stomachs

It's a familiar idea that writing tasks that are relevant to students' real lives can bring out expressive skills that even students themselves may not know they have—and what could be more relevant to real life than eating? In this activity, students practice and refine their use of strong verbs, sensory descriptions, and concise language by writing menu items.

I begin by reading several items from the menus of some popular local restaurants. Then I give students copies of one or two of the menus, or project transparencies I've made of one or two of them, and we discuss briefly (1) what makes the menu item "work"; and (2) how it is structured (i.e., not a sentence, normally). I explain that class members will write menu items intended to make stomachs growl and mouths water.

Next I tape ten or fifteen laminated food pictures (from *Gourmet, Southern Living*, or cookbooks with color photos) to the wall or chalkboard, and number them. Students (either working alone or with a partner) then circulate and select three dishes to write up as menu items: one main dish, one dessert, and one other item (salad, hors d'oeuvres, etc.). They name each of their dishes (as in "Scallops Diablo") and describe them menu-fashion in ten or twenty additional words.

Students can usually finish at least one item in ten minutes. The teacher can either write along with the students or circulate to hear students' ideas on their writing.

Then two or three volunteers each read one of their menu items to inspire further efforts from their classmates. Students continue writing, finishing all three.

We spend the final ten minutes of the class reading and sharing our items, and students comment about which menu items were especially effective, which dishes would be good for a fancy night out with someone special, and whatever else interests them.

Hint: Although this activity works anytime, it's all but overwhelming right before lunch. Bon appétit!

Jim Brewbaker, Columbus College, Columbus, Georgia

Stories in the News

Many times the creativity that we know is in all students seems to be "blocked" when they try to write. Here's an idea that will provide just enough of a stimulus to set that creativity free.

After your students have used newspapers for reading activities, and before you take them to the recycling bin, have students find a couple of interesting articles that intrigue them. After you have encouraged them to understand the who, what, where, and when of the situations described in the articles, try to get students to imagine what the main characters in

the article are really like. Ask them to list some adjectives to describe the character or characters. Obviously, they are only guessing what the characters are like, but what is important is the way they perceive them.

Next, ask the students to come up with some things that might have happened before the incident and list them. Then have the students brainstorm ideas about what dialogue might have taken place before and during the incident. Finally, have the students create their own stories about this incident using all the details and dialogue they have created.

You may be surprised at how inventive your students can be with these stories. Some of the best writings I had last year came from this idea. Everyone who has had "writer's block" ends up with an idea, and all students can create their own interpretations of what they feel really happened. And best of all, the students experience success.

Janice Mulvany, Arvada West High School, Arvada, Colorado

Pitch in to Writing

Some time ago, during a course in the psychology of the gifted learner from the University of Wisconsin–Madison, I heard a professor discuss unusual writing techniques used by professional authors. He described to us the way Fran Striker, the creator of the Lone Ranger, decided on story ideas. Striker used a dart board on which stock western character types were printed (e.g., grizzled prospector, town sheriff, etc.). Whenever he was beginning a new story, Striker would throw two or three darts at the board, and his story would be developed around the characters selected.

A somewhat modified version of this writing technique has fascinated my ninth-grade students for several years. After the class has studied the elements of the short story and has read several examples, the students spend fifteen to twenty minutes during the next class period brainstorming possible *story characters* and covering a chalkboard with their selections. An interesting variety usually appears: cartoon characters mingle with historical figures, famous and infamous living celebrities, and stereotypical characters. The only restriction to the list is that the students may not use their real classmates and teachers as characters. (We also discuss libel and character assassination!) Another chalkboard is filled with equally diverse and imaginative ideas for the *times* and *places* of the stories.

The students then take turns "pitching" at the board. (I use a random drawing to decide on the order they will go in.) Since flying pointed objects and high school freshmen are not a good combination, we use a different procedure for selection: each student tosses an eraser at the board. Whatever character, time, or place is struck must be used in his or her story. A class referee is chosen to decide all disagreements as to which choice was hit (and to rewrite any items that are erased by frequent hits!). Each student hits three to five characters, one time, and one place, which will then form the basis of his or her story. Some interesting combinations develop: a nerd, an absent-minded professor, and a punk rocker in ancient Egypt; Prince Charles, Ronald Reagan, and the Easter Bunny in Siberia on Friday the thirteenth. The more outlandish the combination, the more creative and inspired the students become.

I have used this lesson with many different classes, and the students all enjoy it and create some of their best writing of the year.

[**Warning:** The first time you attempt this activity your principal, superintendent, department chair, and numerous visiting dignitaries will wander by your door. You may spend considerable time explaining that they are witnessing creation, not chaos!]

Karen A. Steiner, Webb High School, Reedsburg, Wisconsin

Memory Chain

I can't recall where I came across this idea, but I have used it successfully as a writing prompt for all ages from eighth graders through experienced teachers in a writing project. The depth to which they extend their pieces varies, but the writing is invariably interesting.

I begin by asking students to close their eyes and relax. I then read aloud the series of prompts shown on page 12, without the numbers or the introduction. I pause to the count of 30 or more after each prompt. Students remain quiet with their eyes closed, letting the ideas come to them but not yet taking any notes. The wait may seem interminable, but it is important. A writing project participant this past summer said she thought the wait time was too long as we did this "prewriting," but that once she started to write, she was delighted with how smoothly and easily the writing flowed. She decided the wait was vital.

At the end of this "prewriting," I ask students to open their eyes and I hand out the instructions and list shown below. On a separate piece of paper, students are asked to jot down words or phrases for each of the prompts. This list becomes the "treasury" from which they draw as they write.

Memory Chain: An Important Person in My Life

Use each of the suggestions below to jot notes to yourself. When you have completed numbers 1 through 15, use this treasury of information to write a good paragraph (probably close to a page) about that person and his or her importance to you.

1. Think of a person who was important to you in the past. The person may be living or dead, a relative or a friend.
2. What is the person's name?
3. Describe a distinctive characteristic of this person.
4. Think of a time when you were with this person. Where were you? Describe the exact place.
5. In your mental picture, what do you see around this person (objects, etc.)?
6. What colors do you associate with the person and the place you are picturing?
7. What sounds (either near or far off) do you recall hearing?
8. Do you remember any smells or fragrances?
9. Were you two alone or were there others present? If other people were present, who were they?
10. What was going on or what were you doing?
11. What did this person typically say? Think of some of the exact words or phrases the person often used, and write them down, including quotation marks.

12. What did you say when with this person? Again, use quotation marks.
13. What do you remember feeling?
14. As you look back, what is your dominant impression of this person?
15. In retrospect, what does that person or time mean to you now?

Look over your notes, add material, and reorganize as necessary. Then write!

Once the "treasury" is complete, students begin a rough draft of the actual piece. For some, this takes the form of a narrative; for others, it is a poem or story. The diversity of genre is encouraged. Rough drafts are shared with a partner or writing group, revised, and polished to be turned in.

For my students, the resultant writing ultimately becomes part of an autobiography which we work on the entire year. Whatever the form the writing finally takes, the prewriting and note taking draw on writers' own rich resources of memory and meaning.

Lucia Leonardelli, Gull Lake Middle School, Kalamazoo, Michigan

F.A.L.L. into Literature: A First- and Last-Line Approach to Reading and Writing

As a lover of literature and a lifelong writer, I always try to find ways to draw my middle school students into reading and writing.

Recently, while going through the bargain-book shelves at a local bookstore, I found an intriguing title: *In the Beginning—Great First Lines from Your Favorite Books* (collected by Hans Baven, San Francisco: Chronicle Books, 1991).

As I leafed through the volume, picking out the first lines of many of my favorite works of literature, I realized that many of the first lines were evocative in and of themselves. Reading the first lines of unfamiliar works, I found myself thinking about what sorts of plots might be developed from these opening lines. Intending to satisfy my curiosity at the library, I pulled out my notebook and copied down the unfamiliar lines I was particularly intrigued with, noting also the titles of the books these lines were taken from.

Then it hit me. If first lines were so intriguing to me, why not use the same interest to motivate my middle school students to do some reading and writing?

I selected seven first lines from works I felt confident the students hadn't read, but which I felt would be accessible and age-appropriate reading:

1. "Serene was a word you could put to Brooklyn, New York."
2. "Early in the spring of 1750, in the village of Juffure, four days upriver from the coast of The Gambia, West Africa, a man-child was born to Omoro and Binta Kinte."
3. "Somewhere a child began to cry."
4. "Now she sits alone and remembers."
5. "The law, as quoted, lays down a fair conduct of life, and one not easy to follow."
6. "I look at myself in the mirror."
7. "Jose Palacios, his oldest servant, found him floating naked with his eyes open in the purifying waters of his bath and thought he had drowned."

I reproduced these quotes on a worksheet (see page 15) and distributed copies to the class. The students were given a chance to read through the quotes and decide which particularly intrigued them or raised questions for them. When they had a chance to review the first lines on their own, they shared their initial reactions. Among their comments were:

"That quote about Brooklyn must be from some really out-of-date book. 'Serene'—Are you kidding?"

"Is Juffure a real place in Africa? I'm going to look it up."

" 'She sits alone and remembers'. . . that's my grandma. She's always talking about what happened long ago."

"That Jose quote could be the opening of a detective story."

" 'A child began to cry.' Is that a book about Bosnia?"

As they talked, the students "sparked" writing ideas from one another's comments. They discussed which quotes were suggestive of mystery (#7) and/or horror (#6 and #7). Also they speculated that quotes #1 and #2 were from stories in which geography played an important role.

After the students had shared their initial responses to these first lines, I invited them each to choose the first line they found most inspiring and to follow it up by writing a first paragraph for that book. Students had about 15 minutes to develop paragraphs that followed logically from their chosen lines.

First Lines

NAME _____ DATE _____

Instructions: The following are the first lines from seven famous books. Read them through first and list any questions or reactions you have to them.

1. "Serene was a word you could put to Brooklyn, New York."
Questions/Reaction_____

2. "Early in the spring of 1750, in the village of Juffure, four days upriver from the coast of The Gambia, West Africa, a man-child was born to Omoro and Binta Kinte."
Questions/Reaction_____

3. "Somewhere a child began to cry."
Questions/Reaction_____

4. "Now she sits alone and remembers."
Questions/Reaction_____

5. "The law, as quoted, lays down a fair conduct of life, and one not easy to follow."
Questions/Reaction_____

6. "I look at myself in the mirror."
Questions/Reaction_____

7. "Jose Palacios, his oldest servant, found him floating naked with his eyes open in the purifying waters of his bath and thought he had drowned."
Questions/Reaction_____

Now select the one that touches you most and follow it up by writing the rest of the first paragraph for this book.

When the students finished writing, I encouraged them to respond to one another's writings. Many students expressed support and admiration for one another's writing. Because only seven quotations had been offered, many students had written first paragraphs for the same quotations, and students were fascinated by the variety of paragraphs that had been written for the same first line.

The session ended with students asking me to reveal who the authors were and what books the first lines were from, which I did:

1. Betty Smith, *A Tree Grows in Brooklyn,* 1943
2. Alex Haley, *Roots,* 1976
3. Elie Wiesel, *Dawn,* 1960
4. Carlos Fuentes, *The Old Gringo,* 1985
5. Rudyard Kipling, *The Man Who Would Be King,* 1888
6. James Baldwin, *If Beale Street Could Talk,* 1974
7. Gabriel Garcia Marquez, *The General in His Labyrinth,* 1989

My reward was watching the students copy down the sources of their favorite first lines and hearing them say they wanted to read the books.

As a result of this initial success, I decided that since the students had enjoyed working "forward" from the first lines so much, they might also respond to the challenge of "falling back" into literature by working backward in plot from the last lines of literary works. But this time, rather than create my own worksheet of last lines from literary works for them, I asked each of my students to select the last line from a favorite book and write it on a piece of paper. They were given two days and asked to select books whose last lines would not be easily identified by their peers (in other words, not a recent class assignment or a book that "everybody" had just been talking about).

When the students came to class with their selections on slips of paper, I distributed a small envelope to each student. I asked students to write their names on the front of the envelopes and place the slips inside. Then I had the students seal the envelopes. One student collected them and redistributed them so no student received his or her own envelope back.

Next, the students opened their envelopes and then proceeded to "fall back" from the enclosed last lines into the plots that preceded them. Once the students had written their last paragraphs, they shared them with the student whose name was on the envelope. The student who had chosen the book then revealed how close the invented ending was to the actual last paragraph. (Since many students are curious to compare their endings to the original, you might want to ask each student to photocopy or write down the actual last paragraph of the book they selected and to bring it to class at the same time they bring their slips of paper.) The students shared the titles and authors of their last lines with one another. Again they were eager to exchange works so they could read each other's authors.

These strategies were also used by my students as peer teaching and parent-child workshop strategies. The envelope approach proved particularly popular since every student was both a preparer and a participant.

As a consequence of this "collaboration" with the actual writer of a particular piece, students become accustomed to the roles of reader and author—good roles to "F.A.L.L." into.

Rose Reissman, Office of Instructional Technology, Brooklyn, New York

A slightly different version of this article appeared in the book, *The Evolving Multicultural Classroom,* by Rose Reissman, published in 1994 by the Association for Supervision and Curriculum Development, Alexandria, Virginia. Copyright 1994 by ASCD.

Introducing Diversity

We all know how strange the first week of a new school year can be, as students and teachers alike adjust to classrooms full of new faces and personalities. An activity like this one, which encourages students to communicate with and start to appreciate one another, can make a real difference.

During the first week of school, the teacher introduces himself or herself to the students by demonstrating how to construct a web (cluster) of his or her favorite recreational activities, hobbies, pets, family members, favorite foods, music, and any other individual interests. The students are then given the opportunity to develop their own personal webs.

The next step is to pair students off with classmates with whom they are not well acquainted. These student partners interview each other, noting ways in which they are alike and ways in which they are different. Their findings are incorporated into a Venn diagram to graphically illustrate their personal and cultural similarities and differences. These prewriting activities serve to set the stage for subsequent tasks.

On the next day, the new acquaintances collaborate to write two paragraphs. They describe their own personal characteristics, but they also compare and contrast themselves with each other. Building upon their prior analysis, one student writes about their differences while the other student focuses on their similarities.

Using the previously written paragraphs as their guides, the students introduce each other to the class. At this time, the teacher photographs the pair of students. Their final compositions, along with their pictures, are displayed on a giant classroom bulletin board to share with all classes.

This activity incorporates all stages of writing, interviewing and oral presentations, and listening skills. It is a terrific way to help students become more comfortable listening, speaking, writing, and presenting. Developing an appreciation for others is another positive outcome of this exciting cooperative learning experience.

Carol S. Pickler, Union Park Middle School, Orlando, Florida

An "Art Gallery" Writing Exercise

To practice developing characters and using dialogue in a short story, our high school class begins by viewing seven interesting prints obtained from the National Gallery of Art: *Unemployment* (Kollwitz), *Cape Cod Evening* (Hopper), *The Dead Toreador* (Manet), *Child in a Straw Hat* (Cassatt), *The White Girl* (Whistler), *A Friendly Call* (Chase), and *Picking Flowers* (Renoir). (Other works that include human figures could be used in addition to or instead of these works.)

Students are asked to view all the paintings closely, then return to the painting that "tugs" at them, jotting down, in their journals, ten to fifteen things that they see in this work.

Next, I pass out a "Creating Characters" worksheet and ask students to select one of the people in their painting to use as the focus for character development. They are asked to supply the following information:

1.   What is the character's name?
2.   Where does he or she live? (Address? Village? City? State?)
3.   Describe his or her home.
4.   What has been his or her education?

5. What is his or her family background? (Parents? Siblings? Names? Ages? Relationships with one another?)
6. Where does this character work? Doing what?
7. If he or she doesn't work, why not?
8. Who are this character's friends?
9. What are his or her hobbies? Interests? Skills?
10. Describe him or her physically, including favorite style of clothing.

After students have fully developed their characters and introduced them to the rest of the class, I give them the following guidelines:

1. Create a short sketch or story using the character in your painting. Ask yourself:
   - What has just happened?
   - What happens next?
   - What sort of conflict has developed for this person or among other people in the painting?
   - Where might this conflict lead?
   - How might this conflict be resolved or settled?
   - What will be the final outcome?

2. In your story, include some of the information from your characterization worksheet.

3. Use dialogue to develop the action in your piece.
   - When you write dialogue, begin a new paragraph every time the speaker changes:

     "Hello, mates," said Captain Handy softly. "What can I do for you now?"

     "You can turn over the ship to me," replied the first mate, his voice filled with tension.

     Handy looked with deliberation at the crowd of mutineers. "So, it's mutiny, is it, you cowards? You can't get away with it!" he roared.

     "We have got away with it, sir," replied the mate.
   - Set off introductory words (yes, no, well) and direct addresses (Jim, Mom) with commas.
   - Punctuate dialogue correctly.

4. Your story should be a minimum of two typed pages long. We will share some of our writings in class.

Students respond to this exercise with interest and imagination, and develop a fascinating variety of narratives from these paintings.

Scotti Miller Jencks, John Stark Regional High School, Weare, New Hampshire

Using Picture Books to Stimulate Writing

Most children begin their acquaintance with reading and writing by viewing stories told largely through pictures. Parents read to them from *Mother Goose, Little Golden Books,* and similar collections in their earliest childhood; and the primary grades continue their usage, since students' response to reading is stimulated by illustrations that allow them to visualize the movements, dialogue, and personalities of an array of characters.

Yet postprimary grades abandon the use of such books and thus lose a vital and colorful stimulus to creativity. Picture storybooks do more than tell a tale; they make settings come alive and add vivid representations that dramatize the writing. They also serve as a catalyst that can suggest and stimulate creative writing. Because each picture evokes a different vision from each observer, the student looking over a series of pictures in sequence is given a powerful pictorial incentive to create a story in his or her own prose to accompany such scenes.

Organizing a picture-book writing assignment is easy and productive. To create an environment conducive to sharing and comparing ideas, I break my classes into small groups of three or four students and have them sit facing one another, all equipped with books of their choosing. Students might bring in their favorite picture books to exchange, or the teacher can offer a selection of richly illustrated books selected from different age levels. Acclaimed books that can spark students' creativity include Karen Ackerman's *Song and Dance Man,* illustrated by Stephen Gammell (Alfred A. Knopf/Dragonfly Books, 1992); Eve Bunting's *The Wall,* illustrated by Ronald Himler (Clarion Books, 1990); Nancy Ekholm Burkert's *Valentine and Orson* (Farrar, Straus and Giroux/Floyd Yearout Books, 1989); Lucille Clifton's *Three Wishes,* newly illustrated by Michael Hays (Doubleday Books for Young Readers, 1992); Lauren Mills's *The Rag Coat* (Little, Brown, 1991); Nancy Ruth Patterson's *The Christmas Cup,* illustrated by Leslie Bowman (Orchard Books, 1989);

and Amy Tan's *The Moon Lady,* illustrated by Gretchen Schields (Macmillan, 1992). (Picture books with or without prose may be used, as long as any text is covered up.)

Students need not use the entire book, but should use between five and ten pages, in sequence, from anywhere in the story. I also become a member of a group and participate in the writing assignment. But first, I write the following guidelines on the chalkboard:

Writing Workshop

1. Take ten minutes to look through your book and fifteen minutes to write a short story about any one of the characters in it.

2. Be sure to give your character a name and your story a title.

3. Make sure your story follows a sequence of pictures from your book.

4. Have your character communicate with others in your story.

5. Your story should have a beginning, a middle, and an end.

After everyone in the group is finished writing, each member shares his or her story by reading it to the group while turning the pages that illustrate the prose. (This will usually take well into a second class period.)

After all the students have presented their pieces, they begin revisions. Students in the group are asked to comment on what they liked about each story and to help point out any possible revisions. Students are encouraged to comment on the titles and characters, and on whether they felt the stories followed the pictures the writers chose from their books. They are also advised to help their peers locate any spelling or grammatical errors, as well as to ensure that each member of the group followed the five writing workshop guidelines. Together, they select one story to be presented to the entire class. The pieces are then saved in student folders for further revisions during a later assignment.

Not surprisingly, many first efforts are both creative and entertaining. Given the proper stimulus, students can produce writing that exhibits great ingenuity and inventiveness. Many students find the exercise both enjoyable and easy to follow. It teaches them how to work together and provides them with an audience for their work. But most important, the picture storybooks provide students with a set of illustrations to focus and guide their creative writing.

Richard Gaspar, Pasco Comprehensive High School, Dade City, Florida

Diaries for Active Reading

Always searching for ways to get my seventh-grade students involved in active reading, I developed the "diary" project. Because my students are offered a choice of novels dealing with issues that affect teenagers, they quickly become interested in keeping diaries written from the perspective of the novels' protagonists. Each student's diary entries reflect not only events in the book but also what the character is thinking and feeling. Students may also create invitations, medical records, photographs, letters, notes, souvenirs, and newspaper articles to be incorporated into their diaries.

The students not only get involved in their reading; they also gain a much better understanding of point of view, as many of them write their first-person diaries from third-person narratives. Imagine my pleasure when a spontaneous discussion began about the virtues of first-person versus third-person narration. The consensus of my seventh graders? They prefer the intimacy of first person because they feel more involved in the story.

The students enjoy putting the diaries together and sharing them with each other, and I enjoy reading them. Here's how the activity is organized: First, each student selects a work of fiction from the library dealing with one of the following:

1. family relationships
2. friendship
3. health issues
4. drugs and alcohol
5. death and dying
6. human rights

Next, students are given the following points to keep in mind:

1. Pretend you are the protagonist. Keep a diary of your life. Remember, a diary contains not only what happens in your life but also how you *feel* and what you *think*.
   a. You should make an entry in your diary approximately every twenty pages. (If your book is a hundred pages or less, you should make an entry every ten pages.) However, you do not need to stop in the middle of a chapter to make an entry.
   b. Write your diary in the first person.

    c. This is not a book log. It is a finished product. Therefore, you will want to allow yourself time to revise and edit your diary before you hand it in.

    d. You can make your diary look like a diary without having to go out and buy one for this assignment, if you use your imagination. Add whatever details you think will let your reader know right away that this is a diary.

    e. Feel free to include photographs, medical reports, letters, notes, souvenirs, invitations, newspaper articles, etc.

2. Plan your schedule: You should read ten pages every night! If you know you have other obligations on some nights, read extra pages on the nights you do have available.

3. Fill out the following schedule to hand in before you begin:
   School library visit on:
   First third of book due (60 pages or less):
   Next third of book due (60 pages or less):
   Last third of book due (60 pages or less):
   (If you have more than 180 pages in your book, see me.)
   Work on editing and revising your diary by:
   Finished product due:
Student's name (print) _____
Student's signature _____
Parent's signature _____

Stephanie P. Radus, Merrick Avenue Junior High School, Merrick, New York

Inferring Character Traits

This variation on a familiar strategy can be very useful in writing workshops. It helps stimulate the students to develop characters more fully in their writing.

I fill an old travel bag with many odds and ends: cards, mouthwash, paper and pens, earplugs, a book, a foreign language dictionary, a blank computer disk, a cassette of offbeat music, denture cleanser, etc.

Next, I take the bag to school and tell my class, "Today we're all going to be Sherlock Holmes. Let's see if we can tell what this person is like from the contents of this bag."

As I pull the items out of the bag, the students keep a list of what is found. I play the cassette for them. We talk about the things we can infer about the person, and what his or her personality must be like.

Next, I ask students to write descriptions of the owner's character. They also draw pictures of what they think the person looks like. The many possibilities suggested by the objects in the bag don't need to be resolved into one single "right" answer. There may be as many different descriptions as there are students in the class, but the main idea still comes across—that these small details can create vivid images of what someone is like.

The next time students are preparing for descriptive or creative writing, I remind them of all the different things they were able to say about a complete stranger. I urge them to build the characters they create in their stories with the same attention to detail.

The students really enjoy this activity. It's unbelievable how many of them are still speculating about our mysterious "friend" days later!

Sabrina H. Williams, White Knoll High School, South Carolina

Computer-Generated Book Reviews

As a first-year teacher, I assigned written and oral book reports. Students hated writing the reports as much as I hated grading them. The second year, I tried reading contests. But we just kept score, and who knows if the students ever really read all those books? Each year I tried something different, trying to inspire my students to read.

Then last year, as I was reading a book review in the newspaper, I found myself asking a frustrating question. *Where do book reviewers learn how to write reviews?* More to the point, how do book reviewers get the courage to write reviews when, at least judging from my own experience as a student, schools don't teach this skill? I knew immediately that this was the answer to my "book report" dilemma.

Students need to learn how to write book *reviews*, not book *reports*. And they need to write them *for the purpose of sharing them with other readers*. Book reports are dull because they have no purposeful audience. But book *reviews* are to be read by potential readers. Aha!

I searched for model book reviews to show my students so that they could begin learning how to write for readers. The search was in vain; I found only one that was engaging (a review of *The Broken*

Cord by ninth grader Jessamy Millican in *Merlyn's Pen*, Special Edition, 1993). I approached our junior high school librarian, Dottie Selby, and she joined my search. What she found was an article by Nita J. Matzen called "H.A.R.P. of Joy" (*School Library Journal*, September 1992), describing a system Matzen had used successfully with her students. (H.A.R.P. stands for Hendersonville Accelerated Reading Program.) It's an inspiring piece that motivated Dottie and me to design our own book-reviewing software program for our students.

Dottie enlisted the help of our science teacher, John Parker, who was familiar with Apple's Hypercard. Using the Hypercard software, he designed a simple computer program that would let our students type book reviews to be read by other students looking for a good book in the library. The format of the program would obviously vary a little depending on the designer, but here's the basic format we ended up with for our Book Reviewer program:

> A field comes up on the computer screen; the student types in all of the pertinent information—title, author, and so on. Then the student selects the *type* of book: environmental literature, biography, Holocaust literature, fantasy, historical fiction, adventure, etc.
>
> The scope of the next two fields is unlimited. In the first field the student writes a cliffhanger summary of the book, up to the point of the book's climax, and ends with something like, "If you want to find out what happens, you'll have to read this book." The second field is the student's response to the book. The student tells a little about the author, describes the author's style, and explains why the book was or was not enjoyable. (This is where the teacher finds special gratification; the personal responses are amazing.)
>
> The student may also make a recommendation as to who else might enjoy the book and why.

The book review is kept on disk in the library for all the other students in the school to access. The student or teacher may print out the book review if desired. Most of my students wanted copies of their reviews to include in their portfolios.

The last step is to take a few choice sentences of the summary and transfer them onto a field set up as a two-sided bookmark. The bookmark is then printed out, signed and illustrated by the student reviewer, copied onto bright-colored paper, laminated, cut out, and distributed to other students by the librarian to advertise and motivate the reading of those books.

(This same approach to book reviews could be implemented using paper worksheets that students fill out and leave in a book review file in the library, but the computer approach greatly increases student interest and motivation in reading and reviewing books. I highly recommend finding someone in your school district familiar with Hypercard, or similar software, who can create a simple program like this one.)

From the very first day that I presented the idea to my students, I have not heard one single complaint about "having to do book reports"! Instead, the students are clamoring to go to the computer lab to write. We don't do *reports* any more; we write *book reviews*, because other readers *need to know what we think*. Thanks to all who collaborated with me on this project, the Book Reviewer truly is a "harp of joy."

Lessons Learned Paper

This writing activity never fails to motivate my students to write. By focusing on lessons learned, it touches on a topic to which we all can relate. Here's how I explain the assignment to my students:

> As you near the end of your school career, it is time for you to reflect on the past and recall events and incidents which have taught you something. All of you have learned many things—things besides "book learning." It is this knowledge—the kind not found in books—that is difficult to teach but very important to pass on to other people.
>
> *Live and Learn and Pass It On* by H. Jackson Brown Jr. (Rutledge Hill Press, 1993) is a book of lessons people have learned, from the seven year old who states, "I've learned you can't hide a piece of broccoli in your glass of milk," to the ninety-five year old who says, "I've learned that deciding whom you marry is the most important decision you'll ever make." We can only guess at what prompted these responses, but we have all had experiences that have taught us lessons, and we often share these lessons with those around us in the form of advice.

Your assignment is to think of three pieces of advice that you would share with eighth graders as they prepare to enter high school. Although your advice does not have to focus exclusively on school, do say something on a school-related issue. Your paper will be shared with an English teacher at the middle school, and she in turn will share it with her eighth graders when they start scheduling next year.

In your writing, explain what you have learned and how you learned it. Provide enough detail to make your support clear and interesting. Also, keep in mind who your audience is and what your purpose is. Your three pieces of advice are due tomorrow. We will work on our rough drafts and final writings in class.

Students' finished writings provide a wealth of personal anecdotes and evidence of lessons learned, both serious and humorous. If your students are like mine, they'll share tips and cautions on topics as varied as procrastinating; talking behind someone's back; getting along with teachers; staying organized; keeping chocolate or other meltables in your purse on a hot day; lending personal possessions to a classmate you don't know very well; joining a new school group; and many others.

Karen Wilkerson, Center Grove High School, Greenwood, Indiana

Stories from Me

Here's a familiar scene: the teacher has just asked the class to write a personal narrative or short story. Three or four students raise their hands immediately to complain that they have nothing to write about. Well, last spring I developed a great tool for helping students generate ideas that can be used at many levels and on many occasions.

For this procedure the students will need paper (either lined or unlined); photographs and special souvenirs from home, representing important events in their lives; tape or glue; and a folder or binder. After reading an autobiography together, students are ready to create their own autobiography booklets using the photos or items they have brought. The students should glue or tape each picture or item to a page and write a short narrative or explanation under it. Once this has been done, each student writes a short autobiography to include at the end. After completing the pages, the students bind them in the folders, which they have decorated, and share their booklets with one another. My seventh graders loved this activity.

When students next complain about having nothing to write about, they can be reminded of their autobiographies, which provide rich resources they can search through for experiences and ideas to elaborate upon. This not only helps them to come up with ideas based on the brief stories they have already sketched out: some even think of other, totally new topics by seeing someone in a picture or remembering an event that took place at the time of the photo.

Since writers write more eagerly and more fluently about those things they know, this autobiography booklet becomes a great source for topic ideas throughout the year.

Sandra Thomas, Pasadena, Texas

2 Literature

Our students are reading "texts" all the time, whether those texts are computer lingo, film images, or their friends' outfits. Now if they could only approach literary texts with the same eagerness and confidence! The activities that follow encourage students to explore the richness that literature offers in new ways, by drawing on history or the news media for related examples, by thinking through their own values and experiences to understand literary themes, and by "translating" the literary work into artworks, texts, or performances of their own.

Literary Roundtable

It is always a problem to get the juniors in my English literature classes to draw analogies among works as well as to use allusions to other works in their writing. Comparing themes found in the various works helps. Better yet, a kind of seminar game incorporating role-playing not only gets them started connecting the works informally but also seems to bring results in subsequent writings.

As warm-up before the first time we play the game, each student is asked to write down ten to fifteen thoughtful remarks that might be made by either a narrator or a character in one of the works we are reading. For example, Mrs. Henne-Falcon in Graham Greene's "End of the Party" might say, "Now you children all line up to get your treats. I know you're all going to have a marvelous time. Be sure to keep your feet off the furniture. . . . Stand up straight now." Or Lady Macbeth might say, "We seemed to get caught up in the idea that my husband could be King of Scotland. Perhaps we should have waited . . . if only Duncan had not come to our home on that particular night. . . ." The students don't copy the remarks from the works but rather use their understanding of the characters and their imaginations to decide what might typically be said by a character or narrator.

In class the next day all except the teacher sit in one big circle. The first student, as a particular character or narrator, makes a remark to the student on the left. That second student responds to the remark and then makes a continuing remark to the third student, again to the left, always in his or her chosen persona. The talk continues around the circle to the left. One round in an honors class began as follows:

Student 1: I really thought I wanted to get away from the drudgery and the weekly hassle with Dad, but the prospect of going so far away from home to marry Frank was just too much. (James Joyce's "Eveline")

Student 2: Perhaps you could get your father to change. I was able to convince my husband to murder King Duncan. I admit I later regretted it, but I *was* able to change him. (Lady Macbeth)

Student 3: But you did commit suicide! Surely there was another way. I faced such a disappointment when I realized how some people in the park felt about me. For a moment I felt destroyed . . . but then I knew I must put my lovely fur away and change my outlook. (Katherine Mansfield's "Miss Brill")

Student 4: Well, deary, I have certainly had to be flexible in my dealings with my five husbands. When I was only twelve, I didn't understand the ways of the world. But I've learned that men only love me more if I control them. (Chaucer's Wife of Bath)

My students, even in the honors classes, are often slow and a bit awkward the first day we play this game. It takes at least twenty-five to thirty minutes the first time, and both teacher and students must be willing to tolerate some silent thinking time at first. However, with encouragement, and a few minutes of analyzing the game itself at the end of the first session or two, the results begin to get exciting. There is a tendency at first to attack one another's characters, but as the students gain confidence that type of response occurs less and less frequently. Often someone will even work in a quoted line to go with a character's or narrator's line. Occasionally I have allowed the students to respond out of turn for the last five minutes. That method is livelier, but it does take away the more productive challenge of having to respond to the lead of the previous player.

Students begin to have fun with the game as they gain confidence, and the result for them is a better perspective on the common elements of a body of literature instead of just isolated, unconnected readings. The necessity of drawing on specific knowledge from their readings also encourages the students to do some independent thinking, and, although the connections my juniors make are sometimes a bit far-fetched, they are still stretching their thinking and exploring connections that they might never have thought of otherwise.

Sherry Ohlfest, Portage High School East, Portage, Indiana

Matisse, Paper Cuts, and *The Pearl*

My first reading of John Steinbeck's *The Pearl* somehow suggested to me the images of Henri Matisse's last major work: the huge, brightly colored paper cuts of his celebrated series, "Jazz." I sensed a relationship between these two works—the "simple" parable with its strong images and themes, and the forceful playfulness of Matisse's childhood memories and violent visions.

Our understanding of *The Pearl*, I sensed, could proceed from actively exploring and integrating the texts of Matisse's art and Steinbeck's words. We set out, then, to "re-create" *The Pearl*, both individually and collectively, by creating our own series of "Jazz"-like paper cuts. Through this applied connection, students learned to read text more closely, detect symbols with greater ease, and create an interpretive work of their own for public view.

We began not with visual art or written text, but with music: Joaquín Rodrigo's "Concierto de Aranjuez." For about ten minutes students wrote down the images or settings suggested to them by the music, and then a few volunteered to share their writing with the class. We discussed how one form of art can be connected to another: in this case, the music influencing or suggesting our writing. I then explained how we were going to connect another form of art—Matisse's paper cuts—to our "reading" of the novel.

Our local library had eight slides from "Jazz" in its collection (an alternative source would be a library book on Matisse); I showed these to the class, and urged them to use their imaginations to guess at the titles. Students began seeing the patterns in each work, and their "guesses" grew to understanding as I switched from the slides to other examples (books, postcards, and posters). The conversation moved from titles to composition, colors, moods, and the materials that shaped Matisse's vision in these works. Students loved the bright colors and the dancing shapes.

I then went back to the writing we had done to Rodrigo's music and used some of these images to briefly introduce the setting of Steinbeck's parable. We read the first two pages of the book together twice, to get a feel for its voice, images, and color.

I explained that we would take each of those first two pages, and every page thereafter to the end of the book, and use them as the subjects of our own Matisse-like paper cuts. Students would choose what they felt were the most important images on their assigned pages, and visually translate their understanding of those pages into finished paper cuts. Each student would be responsible for four pages, or paper cuts, each from a different part of the book. We would then arrange these, in order, completely around the walls of the classroom. By following the path of the paper cuts, we would, in essence, both retell the story of *The Pearl* and transform it into our own work of art.

The worksheet shown below served as an initial guide. Four students volunteered to work together and model the process for the rest of the class, fishbowl style. Using page 2 of *The Pearl*, they discussed and answered the questions on the worksheet and negotiated the images and colors they thought should be on the paper cut, and then each cut one or two shapes out of construction paper. From these shapes, they composed their "picture" quickly, and glued the pieces down. The whole process took about ten minutes, beginning to end.

Worksheet

Look closely at the page I've assigned you for your first paper cut. Read it *slowly.*

Get a feel for everything that's on the page. Break down each line and draw out as many images as you can, no matter how large or small. What is described? Is there any dialogue? What names do you find? What colors are mentioned or suggested?

Once you've looked at it a couple of times, answer the following as completely as you can. A more thoughtful response here will help you as we begin doing our paper cuts next week.

1. What is happening on this page of the book?
2. Look for all the images and details on the page. Write these down in a list here.
3. If you had to pick *three* of these images as the three you think are the *most important or telling,* which three would they be?
4. Think about the role this page plays in the book. Why does Steinbeck include the information he does here? What is the main thing you think he wants you to pay attention to in these paragraphs?
5. Colors play an important role in art of all kinds. They can have symbolic meanings, and they create certain moods in the person viewing the art. Reread the page, and note which colors come to mind, either symbolically or literally. Once you've reread it looking for color, write down three colors you saw and also what led you to see those colors.

We reflected on what had happened, and together agreed that: (1) We were not after "great art," but art that reflected our view of what was important on the pages of the book; (2) simple patterns had more impact than lots of small, intricate shapes; (3) more abstract shapes, rather than realistic ones, produced a more Matisse-like feel; (4) the choice of images, colors, and shapes was a very personal matter, and no two people were ever going to come up with exactly the same picture; and (5) we needed more than the basic colors, using bright neons and several shades of Baja California blues, reds, and yellows.

We took other, more traditional approaches to the novel, as well, looking at Steinbeck's background and vocabulary, doing quick-writes, raising genuine questions, and completing basic comprehension exercises. Along the way, we dedicated class time to working on our paper cuts after we had "completed" each fourth of the novel. It was interesting to note how much richer, more thoughtful, and more complex the visual interpretations became as students grew to know more of the characters, the culture portrayed in the book, and the habit of close reading.

Finally, students included passages from Steinbeck's text on the paper cuts themselves. That made the textual basis of their interpretations clear and demonstrated their ability to extract meaning from the novel.

This project took on a life of its own in a way I've rarely seen in my years of teaching. Students were eager to display their understanding of a text in a visual way, and the hands-on approach made their readings come alive. They were excited to see how their paper cuts fit together and curious to see what others had chosen to highlight.

Since I had two classes working on this project simultaneously, we actually created two full paper cut versions of *The Pearl* on the walls of our classroom—one right above the other. Individual works thus became part of the larger wholes, and we were able to compare and contrast those two works at the end of the project.

Neal Modelevsky, Alameda High School, Alameda, California

Six Characters in Search of a Party

I had often struggled with how to make the characters in F. Scott Fitzgerald's *The Great Gatsby* come alive to my high school students. I thought of this idea one day on my way to class, and it has been a mainstay of my *Gatsby* unit ever since. It is an activity that can be done in one class period early in a reading of the novel, and can be adapted to spark the same lively responses to other works of literature as well.

After reading Chapter 3, the marvelous blue-lit party scene, students have been introduced to all the major characters in *The Great Gatsby*—Myrtle, Tom, Nick, Jordan, Daisy, and Gatsby. I divide the class into groups and let each group choose a character. Their task, which can take anywhere from twenty to forty minutes depending on the level of detail you request, is to design a party for the character they have chosen. They must include location, time, occasion, dress, specific foods, drinks, entertainment, and any other details you want to include (for example, a list of five or six modern-day celebrities who would be sure to be invited). Most important, though, the party they plan must be an accurate reflection of the character they have chosen. I warn them that no character is simple, and that the best starting place is the novel, with the characters themselves. The group must arrive at some consensus as to who these characters are before they begin to plan the party.

This part of the exercise never fails to be animated, energetic, and thought provoking. Students argue about whether Tom Buchanan would drink American beer or imported, which they see as a question of whether

Tom is a snob or a redneck . . . or both. They struggle with how to make Myrtle's party tacky despite having all the accoutrements of class—no cheesespread out of a jar for her! And they always enjoy sharing their parties, and their characters, with the rest of the class, in the process learning a great deal about the way authors portray characters and relationships by the skillful accretion of such detail.

The project can be taken one step further, however, especially for older students. For homework, I ask students to write about a moment—a specific scene, image, or action—from the party they have planned, and to do it in a style as close to Fitzgerald's as they can. Whether or not we have discussed style, this exercise is always valuable. Students already feel they "own" the material—they can easily choose a moment in their particular party because the dynamics are already clear to them. The challenge, then, becomes to portray those dynamics the way Fitzgerald would, which means looking closely at how Fitzgerald *does* describe his characters and settings and events. Students spend a lot of time in the text before they even begin to write. Every student has, in the finished piece, a line or two which has the Fitzgeraldian sense of color or sound or repetition. Some students meet with even greater success, writing fluid, jazzy pieces that bring to life a facet of Myrtle or Nick or Daisy.

We read these pieces aloud to each other the following day, and then proceed through the novel with a stronger sense of character and a new eye for style.

Elaine Christensen, Lakeside High School, Seattle, Washington

Revenge in "The Cask of Amontillado"

Ninth graders in our school study literary genre, and during the short story unit we study Edgar Allan Poe's "The Cask of Amontillado." Usually, they enjoy the story as they get involved in its Gothic elements and the typical Poe surprise ending. Last year, however, I decided to get students thinking about the revenge and crime portrayed in the story as well. In order to do this, I prepared a Revenge and Crime Opinionnaire for them. Before I introduced the story, I handed out the opinionnaire shown on page 37 and had each student complete it individually. After they had all completed the opinionnaires, we had a class discussion on their answers and tabulated the results on the board. We paid particular attention to questions that seemed to contradict each other and questions on which students had differing opinions. Almost all of the students were anxious to participate in this activity since they all wanted to share their opinions. In addition, many students were ready to back up their opinions with real-life stories of revenge and its effects. This proved to be an exciting activity that could be adapted to many other stories and themes as well.

The next day in class we listened to a recording of the story. As the narrative unfolded, the students became involved not only with the horror of the story but with the motivations of the characters as well. When the story ended, many hands shot up, and many students mentioned connections between the story and the questions they had discussed the previous day. As part of our class discussion of the story, we then talked about whether any of our answers on the opinionnaire would change as a result of reading the story. In many cases, the students felt that what they had just experienced would make them change their opinions. We also looked at the opinionnaire questions and tried to decide how Montresor might answer and then how Fortunato might. Again, most of the class was anxious to participate because they wanted to compare their way of looking at the issues with the characters' approach.

Because of the high level of involvement in the story, I thought that students would enjoy additional chances to develop and share their ideas. Since the ending of the story is ambiguous, I suggested that they finish the story and explain what happened to Fortunato after Montresor left. Another idea I proposed was to look to the future and explain what would

Revenge and Crime Opinionnaire

Directions: Read each of the following statements. Write *A* if you agree with the statement or *D* if you disagree.

_____ 1. There is no such thing as a perfect crime.

_____ 2. Villains do not always meet with punishment in life.

_____ 3. If someone does something wrong to you, it is right to do something bad to him or her in return.

_____ 4. Some people are able to hide crimes and never feel sorrow for what they did.

_____ 5. Victims of crimes usually do something to cause the crime to occur.

_____ 6. When someone offends you, you must forgive and forget what that person did.

_____ 7. In this world, good is rewarded and evil punished.

_____ 8. Almost all crimes happen on the spur of the moment.

_____ 9. If a person performs an evil deed, that person will suffer pangs of conscience until he or she confesses it.

_____ 10. Many times crimes happen to people who happen to be in the wrong place at the wrong time.

_____ 11. People should be flattered when others praise them and ask them for advice about their areas of talent.

_____ 12. Many evil deeds are the result of carefully laid plans.

_____ 13. If a person has a talent for something, he or she should be very proud of it and let other people know about it.

_____ 14. No person could stand by and watch another person die needlessly.

happen if the house were razed and the chained skeleton discovered. Another possibility would be to determine to whom Montresor is telling the story and why he is telling it at that particular time. Or, the student might choose to switch the point of view and have Fortunato tell the story instead of Montresor.

All of these writing assignments will help students to write descriptively about literature as they learn to think critically and make judgments based on their opinions.

Jan McAuliffe, Mother McAuley High School, Chicago, Illinois

Taking Both Sides

To encourage students to consider a character in a novel from all aspects of that character's personality and circumstances, I ask students to think of three reasons a particular character might evoke sympathy in the reader and three reasons the character might not. Each reason must be supported by quotations from the novel.

I have used this technique successfully with Charles Dickens's *Great Expectations,* and the assignment can easily be adapted for other novels, plays, and short stories. Any of the major characters may be used. The following are abbreviated examples of my students' responses to two of the main characters from *Great Expectations.*

A. EVOKES SYMPATHY IN THE READER

1. Character: Estella
2. Reason: Estella has no choice in her life; she must always do Miss Havisham's bidding.
3. Quotation: "We have no choice, you and I, but to obey our instructions. We are not free to follow our own devices, you and I."

B. EVOKES NO SYMPATHY IN THE READER

1. Character: Estella
2. Reason: Estella deliberately breaks men's hearts.
3. Quotation: "[When Miss Havisham] extorted from [Estella] by dint of referring back to what Estella had told her in her regular letters the names and conditions of the men she had fascinated, I saw in

this that Estella was set to wreak Miss Havisham's revenge on men. I, too, was tormented. . . ."

C. EVOKES SYMPATHY IN THE READER

1. Character: Miss Havisham
2. Reason: Miss Havisham was swindled out of great sums of money by her fiance and deserted by him on their wedding day.
3. Quotation: "He got great sums of money from her, and he induced her to buy her brother out of a share in the brewery . . . at an immense price, on the plea that when he was her husband he must hold and manage it all. . . . The marriage day was fixed, the wedding dresses were bought, the wedding guests were invited. The day came, but not the bridegroom."

D. EVOKES NO SYMPATHY IN THE READER

1. Character: Miss Havisham
2. Reason: Miss Havisham raised Estella for one purpose: to break men's hearts so that she herself could have revenge on all men.
3. Quotation: "Love her, love her, love her! If she favors you, love her. If she wounds you, love her. If she tears your heart to pieces— and as it gets older and stronger, it will tear deeper—love her, love her, love her! . . . I adopted her to be loved. I bred and educated her to be loved. I developed her into what she is, that she might be loved. Love her!"

Students might also find that some characters are deliberately created as "flat," that is, almost entirely good or bad, and then might be encouraged to think about what purpose such characterizations serve in the text. Sometimes, too, readers may infer more dynamic qualities in an apparently "flat" character.

Since different students will have different reactions to the characters, comparing their responses generates a great deal of lively thought and discussion. The activity also encourages students to interact with the literature beyond their initial reading, and to gain greater insight into the characters, as they delve into the text again and again for evidence to support or modify their responses.

Claudette Russell, Plainfield High School, Central Village, Connecticut

Tapping Other Media to Reinforce Literary Themes

Last spring while my class of eleventh-grade American literature students was reading Ray Bradbury's *Fahrenheit 451*, we began to discuss whether all science fiction eventually becomes reality, and whether the events which Bradbury relates in his classic are common in our society today. Students began to offer examples concerning the impersonal nature of society, the mechanization of institutions, the lack of understanding of classical literature. Several students questioned whether these events would naturally occur in the evolution of society or whether the author initiates something of a "self-fulfilling prophecy."

I decided to allow students the opportunity to pursue their lines of questioning. I removed the bulletin board display and asked the students to find magazine articles, newspaper articles, political cartoons, advertisements, or written summaries of items they heard on news broadcasts. Even sensational magazine programs such as *A Current Affair* or *Hard Copy* were acceptable sources. I then posted on the bulletin board in large letters *Fahrenheit 451 . . . America 1994???*. I promised students extra points for participation if they submitted articles or cartoons.

I certainly did not have long to wait: articles, summaries, and cartoons began arriving promptly the following day. What a diverse media blitz we had! Students had found illustrations of the dehumanization of society, the profusion of special-interest groups, the tragic consequences stemming from the denial of self-discipline or ethical choices. The offerings ranged from the simple news "blurb" to the subtly sophisticated cartoon, from the bizarre to the tragic, from the outrageous to the hilarious. I began to notice the students adopting a real "ownership" in the study of the novel, and almost all students congregated around the board daily to read and discuss what new items had been added since the day before. Amazingly, two students were waiting for me on registration day this fall to discuss the similarities in Montag's flight to freedom and O. J. Simpson's highly publicized trip around the L.A. expressway system!

Having seen the way this strategy bridges the separation between the printed page and the real world, I plan to use this approach with other novels, attempting to call attention to the fact that while social trappings may change, people's emotions and actions rarely do. When teaching students how to adapt and to apply knowledge is so critical, this simple cross-referencing of media makes the novels live. It brings the abstract notion of *theme* into connection with real events, providing the opportunity to discuss the results of actions and the differences between choices and ethics.

Janey M. Jackson, Kirby High School, Memphis, Tennessee

"Aroint Thee, Dude!"

Each year as I dust off *Romeo and Juliet* to get them ready for incoming students, I ask myself the same questions: "Is this play an appropriate choice for the ninth grade? Is there any way to make Shakespeare meaningful for these kids?" Each year I answer myself in the same ways: The conflicts are clearly age-appropriate for fourteen-year-olds. The trouble is the language. The same language that never ceases to amaze me with its humor, poetry, and depth is the bane of my students' existence. "Why did that Shakespeare dude talk so funny? I can't understand anything those people say." Then once I have "translated" it (including expressions like "Aroint thee," which means "Begone"), I hear, "If it means that, why didn't he just write it that way?" My struggle to create Shakespeare converts will undoubtedly continue, but I now supplement our reading and discussion with an activity that motivates students to try to close the language gap.

I ask students to form their own acting companies within the class, preferably three or four to a group. I ask them to choose a familiar, contemporary scenario, one we should recognize immediately, such as kids waiting for the bus, discussing a big test, or gossiping about the new student in school. Although the premise should be modern and familiar, *the dialogue is to be written in Shakespeare's language.* I arrange a performance date and some intermediate steps with deadlines, at which points I can review scripts with students and help with blocking. And I offer extra credit for the use of costumes and props in the final performance.

To facilitate the writing, I supply the following checklist of required elements. As a warm-up to group work, it may help students to review these elements in class and look at examples from the text:

- a reference to a Greek entity (hero, god, place, story)
- a simile, metaphor, or personification
- *thy, thee, thou, thine, dost, doth* where appropriate
- at least one expression like *anon, O, counsel,* or *Gooden*
- inverted word order when appropriate

The results of this activity are always interesting, often humorous, sometimes quite good. The process is the key, however. Students become actively involved in looking through the play, reading lines aloud, experimenting with different phrases and constructions, and generally trying to understand similarities and differences between modern standard English and its Elizabethan, Shakespearean counterpart. These are all valuable steps to appreciating the rich language and content in Shakespeare's plays.

Stephen A. Harlan-Marks, Spring Lake Park High School, Minneapolis, Minnesota

Grendel on Trial

In teaching *Beowulf* at the start of a junior-year literature course, it is always a challenge to make the poem accessible to contemporary students who are inclined to utter "Who cares?" in the face of a story written centuries ago.

Three years ago, I began using John Gardner's 1971 novel *Grendel* as a companion piece. It too has appeal problems for today's teenagers (the philosophical ramblings of the dragon and Ork, the priest, are particular stumbling blocks), but the language is easier, the book is relatively short, and, in general, even the least motivated reader finds the shift in point of view very revealing.

Given the fact that *Beowulf* describes one very definite view of the events and *Grendel* a very different, but equally definitive, perspective on the same situation, it occurred to me last year that this was the perfect material with which to hold a mock trial. Accordingly, I assembled a prosecuting team made up of three attorneys, each of whom had the task of questioning at least two witnesses from a list that included Beowulf, Breca, Hrothgar, Wealtheow, Unferth, and a court-appointed psychiatrist. The defense team had its own three lawyers, and a witness list that included Grendel, Ork, the dragon, and their own psychiatrist. Most of the speaking parts were easily filled by volunteers; the remaining students were given roles as jurors or newspaper reporters assigned to cover the trial. I assigned myself the role of judge.

The trial took one full class period to prepare, as the attorneys had to compose their opening remarks and rehearse testimony with their witnesses (once the actual testimony began, attorneys for both sides learned the dangers of not preparing their witnesses). Following the trial itself (which took two 45-minute class periods), the prosecution team had to write a 500-word summary of its case, and the defense had to do the same for its side. The jurors wrote a 500-word essay explaining their verdict, and the newspaper correspondents wrote a newspaper article summarizing the events of the trial for their readers.

Besides the fact that it got students out of the normal classroom routine and made them active participants in a fairly major undertaking, the most gratifying part of the process was watching the "attorneys" frantically search the texts for quotations and references they could use to "shoot down" a particular witness during cross-examination. This kind of spontaneous critical thinking is too rarely seen in today's structured classrooms; as a teacher, I found observing it firsthand without having to intervene or facilitate almost too good to be true!

One other note: as was the case last year, the defense won this year by a 10–2 vote of the jury. While there was no quarrel with this verdict, the students came away with a greater understanding of the intricacies of a criminal justice system in which someone who kills dozens of citizens in cold blood over a period of a dozen years can be found "not guilty" after all.

Barry Donnelly, St. Joseph Regional High School, Montvale, New Jersey

The Modern "Hard Bard"

It was that time of year again—time to read the notorious "hard bard."

"Why do we have to read this stuff?"

"I'll never read Shakespeare again."

"How will this help me get a job?"

"Did people back then really understand his plays?"

"Let's read something *cool* instead."

Complaining or questioning has been the job of the teenager since time immemorial; finding a good answer has always been the challenge of the adult. This time I had one, with the help of brainstorming with a friend: why not show the students that the language of William Shakespeare is timeless?

I began with the two sophomore classes that were reading *Macbeth* and complaining about how hard the play was. The assignment was divided into five due dates, each one matching an act in the play. For instance, four students were assigned Act I; three, Act II; four, Act III, and so on. The due date for the assignment was two weeks after the completion of each act; therefore, each student had an opportunity to read, discuss, reread, and rethink the lines of the poet before attempting the project. The project itself involved the selection of one complete thought from the assigned act that the student thought he or she understood. Then the student was to select a contemporary event to which the quotation could be applied. This event was to be represented in drawings, cutout pictures, or a combination of the two. The quotation, scene, and act were to be mounted on a poster board, which I provided so that all the students' posters would be the same size.

The results were wonderful, ingenious, and insightful, as well as sometimes disastrous. If they were disastrous because of total misinterpretation or because of simplistic or immature representation, students were asked to redo the assignment after an explanation of the problem and after they were able to see the projects of other classmates. Students who are very literal-minded have difficulty with the interpretation of figurative language; however, they eventually find a quotation they can handle appropriately. The learning process takes longer sometimes and is more difficult for some students; the end results, though, are successful. These successful ends I would like to describe. Picture the following representations and quotations:

> One involved a drawing of the face of Tonya Harding, which was divided in appearance. The right half of the face was represented with the corner of the mouth upturned to portray a smile and to enhance the bright twinkling eye. Over the blond hair was sketched half of a gold halo, and the thought coming from the head was a picture of a gleaming Olympic gold medal. The other half of the face had a devilish grin and a dark eye. Emanating from the bottom side of the head was a red devil's tail, and a pointed red devil's ear appeared on the

top of the head. The thought this time included a hand holding a stick hitting a kneecap. The caption read as follows:

"look like th' innocent flower,
But be the serpent under't."
(I.v. 65–66)

On another poster were many photographs depicting the life and honors of Arthur Ashe as a tennis player, a list of his many other contributions to society, a drawing of his epitaph, the letters AIDS, and these unforgettable words, a worthy tribute:

"and good men's lives
Expire before the flowers in their caps, ..."
(IV.iii. 171–172)

There is no end to the coordination of modern event and Shakespearean quotation. For instance, another student drew two young men and pasted on pictures of the faces of the Menendez brothers. They were holding smoking shotguns, while on the lower half of the drawing were the dead bodies of an older man and woman. The caption included these tragic words:

"The spring, the head, the fountain of your blood
Is stopp'd, the very source of it is stopp'd."
(II.iii. 98–99)

All these posters were proudly displayed on the back wall of the classroom to share with the other classes. Understanding current events, grasping the use of figurative language, displaying artistic talents, developing interpretation skills and higher-order thinking processes—these were all a part of this wonderful learning experience.

Barbara A. Ziccarelli, Pascack Hills High School, Montvale, New Jersey

**Using Futuristic Scenarios to Teach
Margaret Atwood's *The Handmaid's Tale***

We all want our students to think about the future, to consider the impact of the decisions they make today and the ways in which they can change the world of tomorrow. Yet most of what we teach is taken from the past.

How can we encourage high school students to begin really thinking about the future? One solution is to use futuristic scenario writing in the classroom. This approach works well with futuristic texts such as Margaret Atwood's *The Handmaid's Tale*.

Plainly, the role of women has undergone tremendous change in recent decades, change that has also, however, met with tremendous resistance. As a prereading activity for *The Handmaid's Tale*, ask the students to learn about and reflect on the role of women in the past. If time permits, they might be encouraged to do research, such as asking parents or other older people how things have changed in their experience, as well as looking into library sources. Also, while considering the portrayals of current trends in publications such as *Time, Newsweek,* and newspapers, the students can consider the role of women in the present. Finally, as a way of imaginatively engaging themselves with the text, the students can begin thinking about what the role of women might be in the future.

Margaret Atwood's tale of a handmaid in the Republic of Gilead is a dystopian futuristic scenario. Before reading the book, students might discuss their ideas of utopias—scenarios that describe the future as socially or politically perfect—before considering the differences between utopian and dystopian futuristic scenarios. Dystopian futuristic scenarios describe the future in negative, sometimes even frightening, terms. Margaret Atwood's *The Handmaid's Tale* is one such scenario because of its frightening message. But students may discover the power in reading and writing dystopian futuristic scenarios because the cautionary nature of such works helps individuals and society to solve problems.

When the students have completed the novel, ask them to reflect on how well they were able to suspend their disbelief and buy into the dystopian world of Margaret Atwood. Ask the students to talk about what value there might be in exploring futuristic scenarios. Finally, invite the students to write their own futuristic scenarios, either utopian or dystopian, that involve the impact of society and politics on women. These scenarios can be shared in class and might be used as one source for more developed written responses to the novel.

In addition, this novel was recently made into a film starring Faye Dunaway, Robert Duvall, and Elizabeth McGovern. For some classes, viewing and responding to part or all of the film may be an option.

J. Loraine Hoffman, Blinn Junior College, Brenham, Texas

For the Young at Heart

If you're like me (a nosy English teacher), you may ask your students to answer several questions about themselves as the school year begins. One of my questions is always "What is your favorite book?" Invariably, several students will raise their hands (it's still the first week so they're rather formal) to inform me that they don't like to read. Of course, nonreaders don't have favorite books. When I tell them to think back to a time when they *did* have a favorite, I am suddenly inundated with titles. *Green Eggs and Ham, Curious George, Mike Mulligan and the Steam Shovel,* and the *Berenstein Bears* are perpetual favorites.

This lively student discussion of children's books led me to create a children's literature unit. There are several components, each of which develops a different skill.

Discussion

Explore the characteristics of children's literature. Include theme, poetry/rhythm, characterization, and any other aspects that seem appropriate to you, your students, and their past learning experiences.

Explore the categories of children's literature. Some categories I've used include information, prereading skills, social issues/themes, reality based, and delight. (This component develops critical thinking skills.)

Critique

Students immerse themselves in children's literature. I provide some books; they bring some from home. Each student keeps a card file of the books he or she has read. On each card is recorded the book's title, author, and illustrator; a brief summary of the book; the student's specific reaction/response to it; the age level he or she recommends for the book; and a rating from zero to ten. I require at least 30 cards from each student. (This component develops reading and evaluation skills.)

Follow-up Discussion

Again we discuss the characteristics of this literature. Now that the students have read some of these books, the discussion is even more meaningful and valuable. They can see the connections.

Presentations

This year my students worked in reading teams to share stories with nearby elementary students. I worked with the elementary school librarian; she was an amazing resource. The elementary school teachers who were interested in having my students visit signed up through their library. To my delight (and my students' minor panic), the list was fourteen teachers long! When my student teams picked their grade assignments, they had to determine an age-level-appropriate book that they wanted to share. Students worked in preparation teams to coordinate projects that would reinforce their story by planning activities for the elementary students linked to the story they were going to hear. *Mop Top* listeners made their own Mop Tops on paper plates with yarn. The kindergarten class that heard *Sam's Sandwich* got to make paper sandwiches complete with their choice of ingredients (including bugs, spiders, and worms) just as in the book. My students brought that class Gummi Worms to have as a snack. The fourth graders who heard *Freckle Juice* got to mix their own from soft drink mixes my students brought in. *All* project ideas were developed by my students. Many of them spent countless hours outside of class preparing their projects, and many of them spent their own money to buy the elementary students snacks and supplies.

As the readings and activities began on the big day, I ran from one class to another; I didn't want to miss a single minute of their great successes. I also took a Polaroid picture of the elementary students with the secondary students, which the younger students could keep in their classroom as a memento of our visit. (Needless to say, this component develops many skills, including organizational skills, creativity, and public speaking skills.)

Reinforcements

My students recorded themselves reading their chosen stories on cassette tapes. We then donated the cassettes to the elementary school library for the kids to check out. My students were thrilled to be called "teachers" and "friends" after only 45 minutes with each class, and both high school and elementary school students wanted to know when we'd return. We designed a feedback questionnaire for the elementary school kids and teachers; we got many positive comments and some constructive suggestions.

Benefits

Students recall a time in their lives when reading was important and precious to them. Perhaps the return of the spark will ignite their excitement once more. They can see and take pride in their maturity as readers—as they reread books they love, they can become re-enchanted or discover flaws they didn't recognize when they were younger. Perhaps most important, they value the importance of positive interaction between themselves and younger students. They are encouragers, active learners, and "cool" role models.

Possibilities

This year, I expanded the unit to include the writing of a children's book as a culminating project. We enlisted the talents of the art students to help us with the illustrations.

Your imagination is your limit with this topic. As we quickly discovered, imagination is limitless when you're young at heart.

Deborah Hansen, Spotsylvania High School, Spotsylvania, Virginia

Connecting with Symbols

During my first year of teaching, I felt quite stumped on how to introduce the difficult concept of symbolism to my tenth graders. I had assigned Nathaniel Hawthorne's story "Young Goodman Brown," and they didn't seem to get much out of it. In fact, they entered the classroom protesting and confused after reading it the night before.

I decided that to help them make the connection between ideas and objects I needed to get them involved with tangible objects that have symbolic meanings. I showed a list of objects and simple line drawings to the students, asking them what meaning each object could represent. I started off with the more obvious symbols and moved on to the ones with multiple meanings. As students suggested ideas, I wrote them on the chalkboard.

Octagon (in red) = stop!
Triangle (inverted) = yield
$ = money, greed, power
Peace sign = peace, the sixties, flower children
ZZZZZ = sleep, tired, drowsy, dozing, naptime

Light bulb = idea, invention, "eureka!"
Yin/yang = Eastern philosophy, balance, harmony
Black cat = superstition, bad luck, mystery, magic
Hourglass = time passing, life passing, aging
Dove with olive branch = peace
Lightning bolt = power, strength, judgment
Owl = wisdom, guidance
Snake = temptation, evil
Colors: Red = passion, power
    Green = garden, spring, abundance, envy
    Blue = peace, sadness
Lamb = spring, youth
Red rose = true love (I briefly explained the language of flowers
that existed during the Victorian era, and how flowers could have
distinct symbolic meanings.)

The greatest thing about this exercise was that it was completely student centered. I just held the pictures and objects up and the students made all the connections for themselves.

Next I turned their attention to the text, in this case "Young Goodman Brown." With our brainstorming activity still in mind, students began to see how an author could be thinking of more than one meaning when choosing names, objects, locations, and details for a story. In "Young Goodman Brown," for instance, they noticed that the traveling companion's staff was shaped like a snake, and they realized that this object could have some significance. My students had discovered that great literature functions on many levels.

Natasha Whitman Ippolito, Army and Navy Academy, Carlsbad, California

Discovering a Community

The opening chapters of *The Scarlet Letter* establish not only the setting but also the essential moral environment in which the action is to take place. In his description of the town, Nathaniel Hawthorne focuses on the cemetery, the jail, and the pillory. Early class discussion of setting concentrates on what these three sites show about some of the essential characteristics of the Puritan community and its views of human nature. Following discussion, students are asked to make a list of places in our own town—Kent, Ohio—that could be used to represent the character and values of the community or groups within the community. Students share their lists and discuss why each place was chosen. Here are some typical selections from my students:

1. The Erie Depot—"The railroad helped to build the town, and the depot was the center of life for years. In its current use as a restaurant and museum, it shows the ability of the community to grow and change."

2. The churches, Hillel Jewish Student Center, and the mosque— Kent's cultural diversity.

3. The Zephyr (a local vegetarian restaurant)—"People in Kent are not afraid to be different."

4. Woodsy's (a local music store which supplies lessons, instruments, and sound and lighting systems)—"Woodsy's represents the creative side of Kent through its role in a strong, active local music scene."

5. Brady's Cafe (the sometimes site of poetry readings)—the strong interest in culture and self-expression in Kent.

6. Kent State University—"Kent has been built around the university and education is a strong value in this community."

7. The library—"Kent is overflowing with knowledge! Five superb elementary schools, one excellent middle school, an honored high school, a university, and the everyday scenes of life all add to the knowledge of the residents of Kent."

8. Williams Brothers Mill—"The imposing structure draws attention to the center of town, the heart of the hard-working community. The mill is one of the many small industries that contribute to the economic life of the community."

9. The Cuyahoga River—"The river looks calm on the surface, yet hundreds of things are going on underneath. In the community, sometimes the hours flow on with no change. At other times, gossip, news and the latest fads ripple through. No matter what, Kent never stops and never quits changing."

10. Fred Fuller Park, Kramer Fields, the bars and restaurants in the downtown area—"People in Kent like to relax and have a good time. This is the fun side of the community."

Each student then selects the three places which he or she feels best represent Kent, Ohio. Next, the students write essays describing the way they see the character of the community by describing and discussing the significance of the selected places.

The discussion helps students to see that setting may be instrumental in creating the atmosphere from which a story grows. In addition, it affords students the opportunity for close observation of the subtleties of Hawthorne's style. Besides encouraging an interest in the community, the writing portion also provides a connection between the novel and an aspect of their own lives.

Mary Knisely Reith, Theodore Roosevelt High School, Kent, Ohio

3 Explorations

In spite of our having to classify what we do by grade levels, subjects, units, and assignments, our experience tells us that some of the most important things that happen in the classroom don't fall into any of these neat categories. A shy student learns to express herself orally, two kids from different backgrounds find out that they both love historical fiction, or the biggest party animal in the class turns out to have plans for nursing school, and you realize that real education is happening here too. The activities that follow offer original ways to help students get to know one another, explore their career plans, appreciate their diversity as a group, and express themselves in the classroom.

Book Reports with Zest

Book reports can be a valuable part of the English/language arts curriculum. They allow students to share their reading with others and to reveal their knowledge and appreciation of the book read. However, by the time students reach high school, they have often developed a formulaic report style: "I read ____, written by _____. It is about ____. I enjoyed it very much. The end." Needless to say, these types of reports lack creativity and defeat the main purpose of book reports—sharing the excitement of good literature with other students.

To move beyond these standard formats, I have put together several book report projects that get students actively involved in their reading. These projects allow readers to express themselves in many ways, including dramatic presentations, creative writing, artistic expression, and persuasion.

These projects also give teachers an opportunity to see students in a new light. The artist gets to show off his skills, while the budding marketer puts on a suit and delivers her sales pitch. Students gain confidence in their English abilities by drawing on their strongest interests and personality traits.

I have found that these projects work well when many or all students have read the same book; the student is able to concentrate on what he or she feels is most important or interesting within the novel, knowing that others are familiar with its basic outlines. It is also entertaining for the students to see what their classmates have done with the same material. In addition to the projects, I usually ask students to turn in brief summaries of their novels as well.

I first tried these projects after my eleventh-grade students had chosen their novels from a list of eight grade-level American classics. The variety of books and presentations that resulted created a lot of interest for the students and made my evaluations very pleasurable; I looked forward to each report, knowing that it would be quite different from the previous one.

The students loved the variety and the freedom of choice involved; I loved seeing them so interested.

The following are examples of some of the most successful projects.

Judging a Book by Its Cover

Design a book jacket for your novel. Include the title, author, appropriate artwork, a brief author biography, and an interesting "blurb" about the story to get the reader interested in reading the book. The artwork should be neat—you may draw it yourself, or you may use pictures cut from magazines. Keep in mind important events, characters, themes, and images. The front and back covers of your jacket should measure at least eight by ten inches, with the two flaps measuring four by ten.

Book^3

Design a six-sided cube that contains scenes from the novel you just read. One side of the cube should have the title, author, copyright date, and publisher. On the other five sides illustrate exciting scenes or major characters from the novel. These may be drawn (with pen, pencil, or crayon), painted, or created collage-style from magazine photos. Artistic expression and neatness will be considered.

Novels! Novels! Novels!

Hurry, hurry, hurry, before supplies run out! This is your chance to show off your sales skills. You will have two to four minutes to present a commercial for your book. Use props and costumes as appropriate. Your goal is to convince the audience that they *must* read your book.

Talk Show I

Two people must read the same novel for this to work. One of you is a talk show host and the other is the author of the novel. You will have four to seven minutes to discuss the novel and its characters in an "Oprah" or "Donahue" format. You should also be ready to answer questions from the audience. The two of you must stay "in character" for the entire skit. You will also need to submit a script outline one day prior to presentation. (This script does not have to be word-for-word; it just needs to touch on the main topics that will be covered.) Costuming and props are encouraged.

Talk Show II

Two or more people must have read the same novel. One is a talk show host and the others portray the main characters of the novel. Directions for production are listed under Talk Show I. Character costuming is required.

It's Alive! Part I

Choose a character from your novel and portray him or her for the class. (Costuming is required.) You should discuss your life and experiences as the reader would find them. (Three to five minutes.) *Become* the character and use first-person point of view; remember, you can't know anything that the character doesn't know. At the end of three minutes, you may take questions from your listeners if you'd like.

It's Alive! Part II

Act out one or two exciting, interesting, or pivotal scenes from the novel. You should have appropriate costumes and props. One day prior to the presentation you will need to submit an outline script that includes the relevant page numbers from the novel. You must follow the events of the novel in your skit as closely as possible, but you aren't required to memorize the lines word for word. One to four people may participate, but all should have major roles.

Kid's Story

Adapt your novel into a children's book. Use appropriate language and illustrations. Your book should be faithful to the story line of the novel, but you may condense or leave out certain scenes or events if they are not imperative to the story. Your book should have a cover, title page, and at least sixteen pages of story. If you prefer, you may use photographs or pictures clipped from magazines for your illustrations, as long as they convey the events in the text. Keep in mind a child's reading ability, vocabulary, and attention span. You may gear your book for kids in preschool through grade 6.

Author, Author

Write a chapter for your book that includes at least one of the characters present in the final chapter. This could be a continuation of the novel's events or could bring in new plot lines, events, characters, or themes. This chapter does not have to solve its own problems, since very few books have chapters that resolve themselves. However, you should leave the chapter knowing how *you* would carry through the plot. Write a brief statement of how you would "wrap things up." Your chapter should be at least four pages long and be written in a style similar to the author's.

Comic Strip

Draw a series of panel cartoons that summarize the novel. You must draw at least fifteen panels, showing the essential parts of the novel from beginning to end.

Book Gallery

Sketch ten important scenes from the novel. Each drawing should measure at least eight by ten inches and should be based on characters, scenes, and events from the novel.

Correspondence Course I

Write a series of letters to the characters in the novel asking them about their lives, their situations, other characters, and so on. Have the characters write back to you. Write a minimum of six letters, each in correct letter form and three-quarters of a page long, excluding the salutation and closing.

Correspondence Course II

Write a series of letters among the novel's characters. These letters can be written before, during, or after the time setting of the novel. Write a minimum of six letters, each in correct letter form and three-quarters of a page long, excluding the salutation and closing.

Makala Vest Witten, Shawsville High School, Shawsville, Virginia

"Please Pass the Fruit-Flavored Gelatin Dessert!"

Fridays are word days in my English classroom. Following the weekly vocabulary test, I engage the students in "word play." During "word play" we study etymologies, figures of speech, idioms, etc. One of my favorite etymology exercises involves the simple words *zipper*, *yoyo*, and *trampoline*. The objective is to show the students how former brand names have entered our language as bona fide words and how some words we hear and use daily are really proper brand names. In advance I collect as visual aids the generic form of each of the following products: (1) an adhesive bandage, (2) transparent tape, (3) a cotton swab, (4) a tissue, (5) a flying disc, (6) a table tennis ball, (7) a plastic foam cup, (8) a resealable plastic bag, (9) lip balm, and (10) a wooden ice-cream stick.

On "word play" day I tell the students that we are preparing to take a quiz. They must follow these directions explicitly: *Take out a half sheet of paper and number it from 1 to 10. You may not ask me any questions,*

and you may not change any answers once they are written down. I am
going to show you ten items. I want you simply to write down the name
of what I am holding.

I then proceed to display each item by walking around the room to
allow for close observation. The students pay meticulous attention, trying
to figure out the catch. Some of them do figure it out after observing the
first few items, but it is too late to change their initial answers. After I
have shown all ten items, my students become very suspicious when I
ask them if they would like to use the grade on this quiz in lieu of the
grade on the vocabulary test they have recently completed. Nonetheless,
usually about half the class decides that the "word play" quiz is an easy
"A." There are many raised eyebrows, then, when I tell them that almost
everyone in class has failed this test miserably!

I then proceed to debrief them. I ask for volunteers to supply their
answers. There is always an objection when I tell them that the first item
is NOT a Band-Aid; it is a plastic adhesive bandage. The next item is
NOT Scotch tape; it is simply transparent tape. The third item is NOT a
Q-Tip; and so on. The students become aware that the items are not
properly called by the names they have written down; however, sometimes they still don't know a product's name because they have been so
well indoctrinated with the brand names. As we check the answers, I
provide the students with information about the importance of companies' protecting their trademarks, not to mention the baffled looks Ameri-
cans get even in other English-speaking countries when we start talking
in this strange jargon of "Kleenexes" and "Xeroxing."

The idea for this activity came from two articles about brand
names. Richard Lederer's "Brand New Eponyms" (*Crazy English*,
Pocket Books, 1989) and Jeff Kunerth's "Generic Use Can Steal a
Brand's Name" (*The Orlando Sentinel*, 8/31/86) provided me with
all kinds of intriguing information regarding this "word play" topic.
Mr. Lederer provides an alphabetical list of thirty-plus product
names that have become "somewhat generic": Baggies, Band-Aid,
Brillo pads, Chap Stick, Coke, Cuisinart, Dixie cups, Frigidaire,
Frisbee, Hi-Liter, Jell-O, Jockey shorts, Kleenex, Kodak, Ko-Rec-
Type, Levi's, Life Savers, Magic Marker, Novocain, Ping-Pong,
Pop-Tarts, Popsicle, Pyrex, Q-Tips, Sanforized, Scotch tape, Styro-
foam, Technicolor, TV dinners, Vaseline, Walkman, Wiffle ball, and
X-Acto knives.

In addition, I always tell the students about the once-upon-a-time brand names that we now consider common nouns (also provided in Lederer's article): aspirin, cellophane, celluloid, corn flakes, cube steak, dry ice, escalator, kerosene, lanolin, linoleum, milk of magnesia, mimeograph, nylon, raisin bran, shredded wheat, thermos, trampoline, and yoyo. Jeff Kunerth's article also discusses the importance of companies' protecting their brand names and how these companies employ services to be watchdogs for the misuse of trademarks such as Xerox, Styrofoam, and AstroTurf.

At the end of our discussion, I ask the students to grade their own papers. I always present the student who missed the most items—there is always one who gets a perfect 0—with the *Brand-Name-Obsession Award.* (Kunerth refers to ours as a "brand-name-obsessed society.") My students thoroughly enjoy this activity and are eager to take home their newfound knowledge. In fact, I have had students conduct similar tests on their own families and friends. Students leave my room with a sense that word etymologies are fun; I enjoy watching their enthusiasm as they learn. But we're still wondering what to call Velcro-like fasteners if we can't call all of them *Velcro.*

Laura F. Yocum, Bishop Kenney High School, Jacksonville, Florida

Persuasion and Nintendo

After my sophomore composition students have completed a unit on "Critical Thinking" and have discussed persuasive techniques such as *appeals to emotion, purr words,* and *elite appeal,* I introduce the following exercise, which draws on students' interest in and experience with Nintendo computer games. Unless all students are familiar with such games, it may be helpful to start off by displaying borrowed game boxes and instruction booklets and to ask students familiar with Nintendo games or arcade video games to describe what a few such games look like and how they are played.

Nintendo Project

Nintendo, Inc., is looking to develop a new game. You (and your partner, if you choose to work with a partner) are in charge of designing one, sketching it, describing it in an essay, and presenting the idea orally to the Board of Directors (your classmates).

First, you need to present a sketch of what the TV screen would look like while playing your game (put this on a blank sheet of paper—use color).

Then, you need to compose a descriptive narrative essay about your game. Your essay should be from four to six paragraphs long. Describe how the game is played, and tell the "story" of the game (most games have an introduction that describes the characters and scenario). Each body paragraph should describe a different "level" of the game. Most games have at least three levels of difficulty, and each level looks a little different and involves different challenges.

Finally, you will present a 2–3 minute persuasive speech to the class, trying to convince us that your game is the best new game for Nintendo. Use one or more of the persuasive techniques we discussed earlier. If you have a partner, you both should contribute *equally* to the speech.

This project will be graded on your sketch, your essay, and the oral persuasive presentation. I will be considering the originality of your ideas, the quality of your essay, and your *attitude* toward the oral presentation.

I have had great success with this assignment. Some of the more memorable games are "Date or Die," involving various "nerds" who are trying to prevent the Prom Queen from reaching the dance; "Meta-morph," where the protagonist is an eagle, a shark, and a wolf in the successive stages; and a game involving numbers that must be "shot down" in numerical sequence.

Doug Nebel, Red Mountain High School, Mesa, Arizona

Involving Students in the Classroom

We all know that active learning happens only with active participation, yet it sometimes takes real effort and creativity to stimulate students to contribute to their own and others' learning.

Encouraging class participation must involve more than simply making sure every student speaks up or dividing students into small groups. These by now traditional approaches are not appropriate for all situations and for all students. For example, I currently have an excellent student who stutters severely. It would be insensitive to insist on his oral participation. I also have some international students whose cultures discourage class participation. At the same time, I have a student who refuses to participate in groups and who won't write a response unless a grade is attached.

Therefore, I'm keenly interested in creative and appropriate ways of encouraging student participation. The rest of this section describes group participation activities that have proven effective for me.

1. Often, each student keeps a community journal in which he or she responds to a reading before class. At the beginning of class, students exchange journals, and then either during or after class, respond to the other student's entry and return the journal.

2. Students place their desks around four chairs in the center. Students come to class with discussion questions on readings, writings, or issues. Four students sit in the center and discuss the questions while students on the outside listen, tapping the participants' shoulders and taking the center seats when they wish to contribute. Class cannot end until all students have been able to sit in the center circle.

3. For parts of the class period, only female students respond, and then only male students respond; or only those whose birthdays are in the first quarter of the year respond, or only those who are wearing socks, etc. Challenge students' creativity by asking them to brainstorm different criteria for who will respond.

4. Jigsawing is an effective group activity. Students count off in fives to divide into groups. Groups generate paper topics or discuss questions; each member takes careful notes. After the allotted time, students count off again, either in fives or using the letters A–E. After dividing into the different groups, each new member shares his or her previous group's results.

   Here is a variation on jigsawing: often, students will not have time to study in their first group and discuss and teach in their new group all on the same day. I have discovered that assigning the first groups at the end of the hour and telling them to prepare on their own before coming the second day to meet in groups allows for better individual preparation. They compare what they will teach with other group members before moving on to the teaching groups.

5. I often put the numbers 1–25 on the board, depending on how many there are in the class. Students who answer questions can then call on other numbers to respond and help them. The numbers correspond either with numbers on my roll or with numbers students receive by counting off at the beginning of the class period.

6. I sometimes have students work on quizzes with a partner. I've found that when grades are involved, students are usually more motivated to work together effectively. On subsequent quizzes, I ask them to work with different partners. This gets students interacting with one another, and as they become more comfortable with one another, they participate more in class discussion.

7. Four students are invited to volunteer as panel members. They are to read two essays, individually, before I meet with the whole panel. During this meeting, we consider the aims and purposes, strategies, audience, and language of the essays. Meanwhile, the other students are assigned to read the same two essays and to write two questions they want answered after their reading. Later, these questions will be directed to panel members. On the day of the essay discussion, I join the audience while the panel members move to the front and direct the class discussion as they attempt to answer student questions. After each essay discussion, I make summary comments, evaluating the panel's and audience's efforts towards self-discovery in reading. (Credit for this activity goes to Colleen Peterson.)

Rodney D. Keller, Ricks College, Rexburg, Idaho

Take Our Students to Work

High school seniors, especially those who may not be going on to college, are often very interested in the opportunities and challenges of the current job market. I ask seniors to complete a research project during the third quarter that gives them a chance to look into these future possibilities. This has been a successful project in that it motivates the students, it teaches research skills in a real-life situation, and it allows business and community members to participate with the students in an authentic way.

I begin by asking students to identify the careers that interest them the most. Once students have chosen the jobs they would like to learn about, I suggest the following guidelines for their use of research sources, and they begin their individual library research.

Minimum Sources to Be Used

1 book
1 magazine or newspaper article

2 reference books (encyclopedia, dictionary, etc.)
2 interviews with people in your chosen career
1 additional source of your choice

Students look into all aspects of the chosen career, including job descriptions, educational requirements, training, salary, working conditions, other people's opinions of the job, and the student's own perceptions of it.

In the meantime I write to the kinds of firms, government agencies, and community organizations in which students have expressed interest, in order to recruit mentors for the students and arrange for on-site visits. Here's the letter I use:

Melissa Awenowicz, English Teacher
South Aiken High School
Aiken, South Carolina 29801

Date, Year

Dear Business/Community Member:

On behalf of South Aiken High School and especially my senior English students, I would like to make a special request. The students are working on a research project that takes them beyond the classroom to apply their knowledge and skills to the "real world," and your help can make this possible.

For this research project each student was asked to select a career that he or she is interested in pursuing after graduating in June. Your contribution to the project would be to allow students to visit your workplace for a day, and to provide a mentor for each student who can show him or her some of the responsibilities of the job. Before they come to you the students will have completed a significant amount of research in the areas of training, job requirements and skills, the job market, and salary, as well as other aspects of the job.

The students will be required to report to your place of business at 9:00 a.m. (unless you indicate otherwise) and remain there until 3:00 that afternoon. Please allow them an hour for lunch, or provide them with lunch, whichever is convenient. While the students are at the site, each of them is expected to keep a log or journal of the day's activities and their impressions. Again, please allow them to be as actively involved as possible in some of the job's duties. In addition to being the mentor's "shadow," each student needs to conduct interviews with two people in the job (one of whom may be the mentor) for inclusion in the final paper.

I would appreciate it if you would also take the time to fill out the attached evaluation form for each student after the visit and return it to me at the above address. It will be very helpful to the students and to me, and will have a bearing on their final grades on this research project.

Thank you for taking an active interest in making education relevant to our students.

Sincerely,

Melissa Awenowicz

Many people are very eager to have students visit their workplaces and to offer whatever help they can as mentors.

Once the students have done some preliminary research, they are ready to visit their mentors at work. Each visit takes nearly a full day, from 9:00 a.m. to 3:00 p.m., and the student keeps a journal of his or her experiences and impressions during the day, which is turned in and included in the grade for the project. The student also interviews his or her mentor and one other person in the workplace, taking notes on the interview to be incorporated into the final report.

Students come to the actual writing of their reports with a great deal of "real-world" information that makes their library research much more meaningful to them. We discuss the content, organization, and format of the report in class, and I give them MLA guidelines for citing sources and preparing the list of works cited. In addition to the written report, each student also prepares a résumé, a cover letter, and a job application for the job he or she has been researching. I explain to students that their grades for this project will take into account all of the following components:

Journal
Report
    proper notecards and bibliography cards
    use of a minimum of seven sources
    outline
    rough draft
    introduction and conclusion
    content
    correct parenthetical documentation
    works cited page
Cover letter, résumé, and application

Melissa Awenowicz, South Aiken High School, Aiken, South Carolina

A Back Door to Characterization

"I'm taping the name of a certain character to your back," the host of the baby shower said. "Now I want you to pair off, letting your partner see your character. The object of the game is to ask your partner yes-or-no questions, trying to guess who your character is. The one who guesses the character first wins."

Well, I didn't win the party game and have the pleasure of presenting the mother-to-be with a sweet little rattle. However, after a heated, but good-natured, argument over whether Tweety Bird is male or female, I did come away from the baby shower with an idea for my classes. What do questions such as "Am I a boy?" "Am I tall and thin?" "Do I have a calm temper?" and "Do people throw rocks when they see me coming?" have in common? They are forms of characterization, of course!

I decided to use this activity to supplement a study of characterization techniques and, at the same time, develop my students' understanding of the characters in works of literature. Throughout the year, in both literature and writing units, we discuss direct characterization, in which we are directly told about a character, and indirect characterization, in which character is revealed by (1) what the character looks like, (2) what he or she does, (3) what he or she says, (4) what he or she thinks, and (5) what other characters say about him or her. Then near the end of a study of a work of literature, we use these methods of characterization as a basis for our questions to discover who we—those characters taped to our backs—are.

Shakespeare's plays seem to lend themselves to this activity because of their complex characters with sometimes hard-to-remember names. Do students know the characters in the play well enough to ask the questions that will reveal identity? One elusive character might be drawn out as follows: Am I female? No. Am I a parent? No. Do I fall in love? No. Do I survive at the end of the play? No. Am I one of Romeo's enemies? No. Am I hot tempered? Yes. Am I Mercutio? Yes!

Of course, much depends on the breadth of the cast of characters, and limits do have to be placed so that students don't simply name off one character after another before reaching the correct conclusion. Minor players are generally not so easily guessed, requiring more knowledge of the work and thus producing more questions.

This "game" provides important preparation for a group project on characterization in which groups of students produce a movie poster for a story or play. Using a recent movie poster as an example, students create a visual that will cause audiences to flock to their production, select appropriate music, write a kicker statement, name their production company and the producer and director, rate their film, and, most important, *cast* the characters from modern actors. (Ours do differ from most movie posters in that students must list who is to play which character on their posters.)

Although group work usually begins with entertaining and preposterous suggestions for characters, students will then knuckle down, deciding that this actor who is typecast as an experienced woman will just not do for a thirteen-year-old innocent, or that this comedian would be perfect except that the audience would be sure to be laughing just when they were supposed to feel the sting of tears. In addition to their favorite stars, students find themselves discussing the attributes of Juliet or Brutus or Lady Macbeth that were brought out in the character-guessing game as they search for the perfect thespian.

I find that these interrelated activities are excellent ways to allow students to see characterization techniques in action in great works of literature.

Kim Fowler, Leopold R-3, Leopold, Missouri

Small Groups with Big Results

Grouping, or working in small groups in class, has become an educational catchphrase for the 1990s. Teachers who have worked hard on developing their own classroom management techniques may shy away from turning their classrooms over to their students, and it is a tough thing to do. But with a few minutes of thought and preparation, any class can easily adapt to this innovative technique for peer editing and collaborative learning. Remember these few points:

Set a Positive Tone

The first step you take toward small-group work will set the classroom tone. Create a positive atmosphere by demonstrating open-mindedness and creativity. Let students know you trust their collaborative efforts.

Find a New Way to Divide the Class

Don't limit yourself in your methods of splitting the class into groups. Distribute color strips, place stickers under chairs, or have the students "Find three people with . . . " Students enjoy the "luck of the draw."

What Happens in Groups?

There are several techniques available specifically for reviewing writing in groups. Two examples are the following:

Pointing:
1. Divide into groups of four or five, comprised of a reader to read aloud and listeners.
2. Reader: Read, pause, and read the same piece to the group again.
3. Listeners: Listen and, on the second reading, jot down words, ideas, or pictures that come to mind.
4. After the second reading, listeners point out what they liked. (*Writing without Teachers* by Peter Elbow. Oxford University Press, 1973)

Say Back:
1. Divide into groups of four or five, again with a reader and listeners.
2. Reader: Read, pause, read again.
3. Listeners: Listen and, on the second reading, jot down (a) what you liked and (b) what you want to know more about.
4. Listeners say these back to the reader after the second reading. (*Acts of Teaching: How to Teach Writing* by Joyce Armstrong Carroll and Edward E. Wilson. Teacher Ideas Press, 1993)

These techniques may seem simple, but they allow the essential components for peers working together. Small-group work also sharpens listening and communication skills, which are transferable to other subjects in and out of the classroom.

Discussion and Evaluation

Allow time for transition from small-group work to whole-group discussion. Discovery time, or whole-group discussion, should be coordinated by the teacher. These discussions are essential for allowing students to make the connections from peer remarks to individual papers. Evaluation of students' work, then, may reflect peer commentaries, group interaction, and overall participation.

Don't be afraid of the "g" word. Asking students to work in groups is not letting your classroom go, but setting the minds of your students free.

Susan B. Cutshall, Eckert Intermediate, Houston, Texas

Fresh Idea from a *Far-Out* Teacher

We all acknowledge the value of dictionaries, but I have found that middle school students do not always know how to use them. Textbooks contain many helpful practice activities to teach dictionary skills, but since students rarely make a solid connection to these activities, I found a more meaningful approach.

At the beginning of class, I announced that students would spend the class period writing dictionaries. After the protests died down, I explained that there were many different kinds of dictionaries: medical, legal, picture, and so forth, each designed for a particular audience. Theirs were to be slang dictionaries. Students started looking more interested.

Next, I turned on the overhead and displayed a slang dictionary I had created circa 1967. I explained the components they too would use in their assignment. Each entry was printed in a darker print to simulate boldface type. The words and phrases were arranged in alphabetical order and each word was divided into syllables. Each entry included a phonetic spelling, an abbreviation for the part of speech, a definition, and any synonyms the word might have.

After questions about and discussion of these components, and when I felt the students understood the basic structure, I gave them dictionaries to use for additional examples. I told them that their own dictionaries must contain at least five complete entries and could include no profanity.

The students thoroughly enjoyed my sharing of slang and even played around with using some of my archaic terms. "Far out!" "Groovy!" and "He's so tuf!" rang out during the day, giving us all a good laugh. Even my least-motivated students got involved in their slang dictionaries. Some students were so inspired they wrote pages and pages. Perhaps most useful was the fact that some of the students who were normally less involved knew the most slang and for this activity became the class experts.

In our multicultural classroom, comparing the different slang terms used by different groups was as interesting and enjoyable as comparing their slang to my "ancient" terminology had been. We all learned, for example, that when someone said, "Wuz up, dawg?" it was not an insult. "Dog" used this way implied a friend. "Fresh" was another word that had evolved. "Fresh" once meant talking back or, even worse, that a man had made an unwanted physical move toward his date. Today "fresh" has the same meaning as the "cool," "groovy," or "tuf" of days of yore.

We displayed the completed pages on a hallway bulletin board. Many other students really enjoyed my class's work and would stop and read between classes. After a week or ten days, we took down the display. We then combined all our efforts, printed our composite dictionary on the computer, and distributed a copy of the slang dictionary to each student in the class.

This activity benefited both the students and the teacher. The students learned about dictionaries and about one another's language; but, even more important, they learned that language arts is not just about spelling, reading, and writing—it is about communication.

Pamela Drury, Olle Middle School, Houston, Texas

Newspaper Reader-Response Counterpoint

Often as I read a newspaper column or editorial, I find myself nodding my head in agreement or shaking it in anger. Sometimes, I grab a pad of paper and write a response which reinforces or refutes the points put forward by the columnist. One day I told my students—multiethnic, inner-city sixth graders—about my habit of responding to newspaper columns, and read aloud my reactions to a Jimmy Breslin column I supported and to a Patrick Buchanan column I was upset by. (The columns presented two opposing viewpoints on multicultural education.) The students enjoyed and even applauded my lively reading of my response, which included line-by-line reactions to the columnist. One student said "You tell him, Ms. R."

Based on their enthusiastic response, I developed a handout to encourage my students to have their own conversations with columnists.

Newspaper Counterpoint Worksheet

Name: _____

Date: _____

Newspaper: _____

Columnist:_____

Title of Column: _____

Topic/Theme: _____

What was the first response you had while reading this column?

Is your first reaction to the column pro or con? Why?

Sum up why you clipped this column. What made it stand out to you?

Write or draw your response here or on a separate sheet of paper.

Now get ready for a line-by-line conversation (friendly or combative) with the columnist. First, find key quotes from the column that you particularly agree or disagree with or are struck by in some way. List them here.

Quote #1: _____

_____

_____

Quote #2: _____

_____

_____

Quote #3: _____

_____

_____

Quote #4: _____

_____

_____

Now go through the quotes and respond to them as though the columnist were sitting by your side. You may want to get a friend or family member to play the role of the columnist and read the quotes.

Columnist's Quote: _____

_____

_____

My Response: _____

_____

_____

Columnist's Quote: _____

_____

_____

My Response: _____

_____

_____

Columnist's Quote: _____

_____

_____

My Response: _____

_____

_____

Follow-up Steps for Students

- Write out your conversation. . . . Refine it! If you want to, mail it to the columnist.
- Look back at what you said. Write your own column, or create your own counterpoint.

Several of my students, after writing their own imagined conversations with columnists, wanted to present them to the class. They role-played their conversations in two voices—their own and a fabricated one for the columnist—to much applause.

Rose Reissman, Office of Instructional Technology, Brooklyn, New York

Get-Acquainted Signs

Since the first day of school is often an awkward time for both teachers and students, I have found these get-acquainted signs to be an easy and revealing way to have students introduce themselves to me and to other class members. I distribute a blank sheet of unlined white paper to each student. Next, I ask each student to draw a sign that will take up most of the paper. This large size helps others to see what has been written as the students hold up their signs and talk about themselves. The sign can be circular, oval, rectangular, or any shape the student's creativity inspires. The only requirement is that it be divisible into four relatively equal quadrants.

After the sign is drawn and divided into four parts, I have the students put the following information into each quadrant:

1. The student writes his or her name vertically in the first quadrant and then thinks up a positive adjective for each letter in the name.
2. In the second quadrant the student draws a picture of what he or she does best.
3. In the third quadrant the student writes the name of the person who has been the most positive influence on his or her life.
4. Finally, in the last quadrant the student draws a picture of what he or she imagines doing in ten years.

When all signs are completed, the class forms a circle and students take turns holding up their signs and explaining the information in each part. This activity takes most of a fifty-minute class period, and by the time it's over, our first-day jitters are gone and we all know each other a little better.

Laura Walters, Calumet High School, Gary, Indiana

Indexes

Author Index

Subject Index